Extreme Habitats

Polar Region
Survival

Jim Pipe

Consultant: Jonathan Shanklin, British Antarctic Survey

Gareth Stevens
Publishing

Please visit our web site at: www.garethstevens.com
For a free color catalog describing Gareth Stevens Publishing's list of
high-quality books, call 1-800-542-2595 (USA) or 1-800-387-3178 (Canada)

Library of Congress Cataloging-in-Publication Data

Pipe, Jim.
    Polar region survival / Jim Pipe. — North American ed.
        p. cm. — (Extreme habitats)
    Includes index.
    ISBN: 978-0-8368-8248-3 (lib. bdg.)
    1. Polar regions—Juvenile literature. 2. Polar regions—Ecology—
Juvenile literature. 3. Habitat (Ecology)—Juvenile literature. I. Title.
    QH84.1.P57   2008
    613.6'90911—dc22   2007006980

This North American edition first published in 2008 by
Gareth Stevens Publishing
A Weekly Reader® Company
1 Reader's Digest Road
Pleasantville, NY 10570-7000 USA

This U.S. edition copyright © 2008 by Gareth Stevens, Inc.
Original edition copyright © ticktock Entertainment Ltd 2007
First published in Great Britain in 2007 by ticktock Media Ltd.,
Unit 2, Orchard Business Centre, North Farm Road,
Tunbridge Wells, Kent, TN2 3XF, United Kingdom

Series editor: Rebecca Clunes
Designer: Sara Greasley

Gareth Stevens managing editor: Valerie J. Weber
Gareth Stevens editor: Tea Benduhn
Gareth Stevens art direction: Tammy West
Gareth Stevens graphic designer: Dave Kowalski
Production: Jessica Yanke

Photo credits: (t=top, b=bottom, l=left, r=right, c=center)
age photostock/SuperStock 23b; Alamy Pictorial Press/Alamy 19t; Arctic Photo 6t, 6b, 7cl, 8–9, 11t, 11cr, 12t, 12b, 13t, 13cl, 21t, 21cb, 25cb, 26, 27t, 27ct; Ingo Arndt/naturepl.com 24t; blickwinkel/Alamy 15cl; Corbis Galen Rowell/Corbis 18t; Getty Roger Mear/Getty 4–5; Jerry Kobalenko/ Getty 10b; Edwin Mickleburgh/Ardea 25ct; NASA 19cr, 25b, 28bl, 28br; Rick Price/Corbis 25t; Rozet/Jupiter Images 20t; Shutterstock 5r, 5b, 7t, 7b, 8t, 9t, 9r, 11cl, 11b, 13cr, 13b, 14l, 14r, 15cr, 15b, 16b, 17l, 18b, 20c, 20b, 21ct, 22t, 22b, 23t, 23ct, 24b, 27cb, 28t, 29c, 29b; Zachary Staniszewski 19b; tbkmedia.de/Alamy 25c; ticktock Media Archive 1, 7cr, 8b, 16–17, 17r, 18–19, 21b, 27b, 29t; Kim Westerskov/Getty 10t; Graham Wren/Oxford Scientific Films 23cb; All artwork: ticktock Media Archive except Cosmographics 26.

Printed in the United States of America

1 2 3 4 5 6 7 8 9 11 10 09 08 07

Contents

Words that appear in the glossary are printed in **boldface**
type the first time they occur in the text.

This map shows the Arctic Circle. Everything inside this circle is considered to be in the Arctic.

Labels on map: United States, Alaska, Canada, Arctic, North Pole, Greenland, Atlantic Ocean, Arctic Ocean, Arctic Circle, Russia, Europe, Africa

The Ends of The Earth

If you are looking for an extreme habitat, head for the ends of Earth. The poles are some of the harshest places on the planet. Bright, white snow and ice stretch as far as you can see into the distance.

Earth has two polar regions. They are the coldest, driest, and windiest places on the globe. Temperatures can drop to a brain-numbing −58 °Fahrenheit (−50 °Celsius).

The **Arctic** is the name given to the area around the **North Pole**. There is no land underneath most of the Arctic. Instead, a giant sheet of ice floats on top of the **Arctic Ocean**.

Arctic explorers should travel light — especially if they have to pull their own sled.

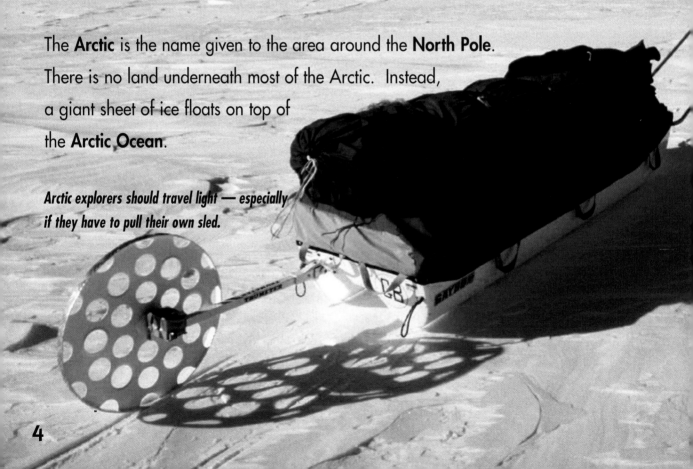

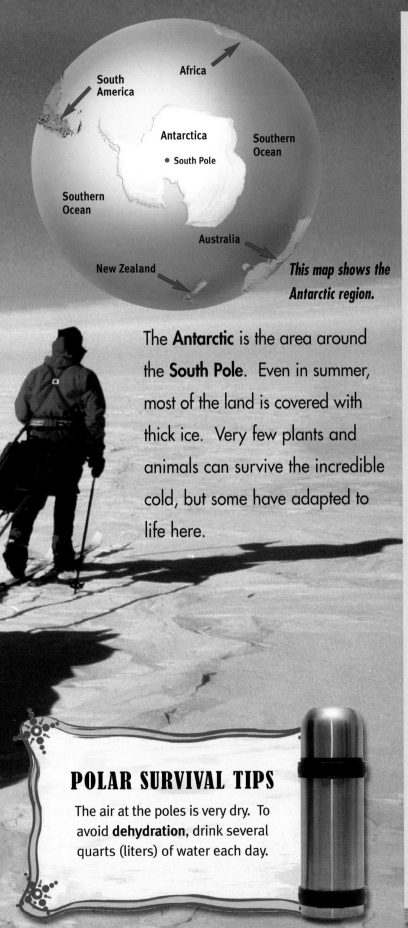

This map shows the Antarctic region.

The **Antarctic** is the area around the **South Pole**. Even in summer, most of the land is covered with thick ice. Very few plants and animals can survive the incredible cold, but some have adapted to life here.

POLAR SURVIVAL TIPS

The air at the poles is very dry. To avoid **dehydration**, drink several quarts (liters) of water each day.

Polar Notebook

- Antarctica is the fifth largest continent. Only Europe and Australia are smaller. Antarctica is one and a half times the size of the United States.

- When temperatures drop to −94 °F (−70 °C), your breath freezes. When it falls to the ground, it makes a noise some people call "the whispering of the stars."

- Compasses work using a needle that points toward the **magnetic North Pole.**

With a compass, a traveler can always find north.

- The magnetic North Pole is about 994 miles (1,600 kilometers) south of the geographic North Pole. This pole is not fixed in one place. It slowly moves its position all the time.

Polar Explorer

*A trip to either pole is like visiting another planet. You can watch giant **icebergs** float by, climb jagged mountains, sail past huge cliffs of ice, or just gaze at the empty, icy landscape.*

In the polar regions, it is vital to stay warm and dry. Wear lots of layers to trap warm air, and cover these layers with a thick jacket to protect yourself from the wind. Choose boots with rough soles and spikes to grip the icy ground.

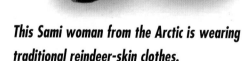

This Sami woman from the Arctic is wearing traditional reindeer-skin clothes.

If you forget to pack your tent, do not worry. An igloo will protect you from freezing winds. Igloos are traditional shelters made from blocks of ice stacked tightly together to form a dome.

Although igloos are made from snow and ice, they are warm inside.

POLAR SURVIVAL TIPS

If you see a skua – duck! Stay away from their nests particularly since these vicious birds will attack your head with their feet.

- When your skin freezes, it swells up and turns black. This condition is called frostbite. In extreme cases of frostbite, the swollen area must be cut off.

Extreme frostbite

- The cold is dangerous. If your body temperature drops below 89.6 °F (32 °C), you could die.

Scientists drill deep into the ice in Antarctica to take samples called cores. They study ice-core samples to learn about changes in the ice over time.

Polar explorers need a lot of equipment. Before you go, make sure you have the essentials:

- Warm clothing and boots
- Tent and sleeping bags
- Food supplies (dried foods are lighter)
- Small cooking stove and fuel
- Rope, ice ax, and snow shovel
- Skis and snowshoes
- Maps, compass, and satellite phone

Use a snowmobile to travel around on the snow and ice.

7

The Coldest Place on Earth

Look inside your frezer. Everything is frozen. Imagine living in an icy place colder than your freezer. The Antarctic is the coldest place on Earth. If you threw boiling water in the air here, it would freeze instantly.

The Arctic tern travels between the Arctic and Antarctic, making a round trip of 21,750 miles (35,000 km) every year.

The Antarctic is colder than the Arctic. The Arctic is warmer because currents of warm water flow into the Arctic Ocean. Warm water keeps the temperatures slightly higher. With warmer temperatures, the layer of ice covering the ocean is thinner than the layer of ice covering the land of Antarctica.

Several species of penguin live in the Antarctic, but only emperor penguins have their chicks during the bitter Antarctic winter.

POLAR SURVIVAL TIPS

Wear sunglasses or dark goggles. Looking at bright white snow for too long can seriously damage your eyes. It can cause **snowblindness,** which is painful and makes your vision blurry.

Polar Notebook

- The coldest temperature ever recorded was in 1983 in Antarctica. It was a bone-chilling −128 °F (−89 °C).

- In autumn, the Antarctic sea ice grows at a rate of 2.5 miles (4 km) each day.

In autumn, this sea will freeze over.

Antarctica is also cold because of its **elevation.** The average height of the area is 8,200 feet (2,500 m) above **sea level**, which is three times higher than any other continent in the world.

- When the sea freezes, Antarctica doubles in size. It takes just two and one-half weeks for this to happen.

Most mountains on Antarctica are buried under ice. Only a few peaks, known as nunataks, stick out.

Why is it so cold?

The poles are cold because they never face the Sun directly. The Sun's rays are weaker and more spread out at the poles than they are at the **equator**.

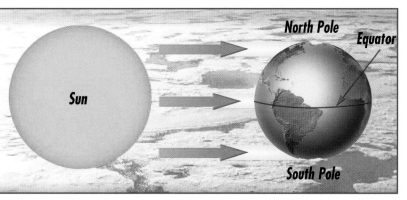

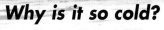

9

The Frozen Kingdom

Almost everything in the Arctic Circle is frozen. The sea in the center of the circle is almost as solid as the land at its edges!

Ships known as icebreakers smash their way through sea ice. The front of the ship is shaped to push it up onto the ice. Then the ship's weight forces the ice to split, creating a path.

In summer, the Arctic ice shrinks. Around the edges of the ocean, the ice breaks into large sheets. These sheets are separated by channels of water known as leads.

USS Healy is used for polar research. Here, it cuts a path through the ice for other ships.

A scientist jumps over a lead in the Arctic.

Arctic scientists uncover their sled after a blizzard.

In polar regions, glare from dazzling snow can play tricks on your mind. You can lose your sense of up, down, far, and near. Pilots crash their planes and explorers fall over cliff edges. Even birds fly into the ground!

In 1997, three skydivers died after failing to open their parachutes. They did not realize they were so close to the ground.

These skydivers wear skis for landing on the Arctic snow.

Polar Notebook

- On average, the Arctic ice is 10 to 16 feet (3 to 5 meters) thick.

- In winter, Arctic ice covers 6 million square miles (16 million square kilometers) of sea, but it shrinks to 3.5 million square miles (9 million sq km) in summer.

- Arctic houses are built on wooden **stilts,** some of which are up to 50 feet (15 m) tall. Without stilts to prop a house up from the ground, the warmth from the house would melt the frozen ground below and the building would sink down into the ice!

Russian houses in the Arctic

POLAR SURVIVAL TIPS

Be careful on the ice! Ice may look smooth, but it is actually rough and can cut you if you fall. Ice crystals look sharp under a microscope.

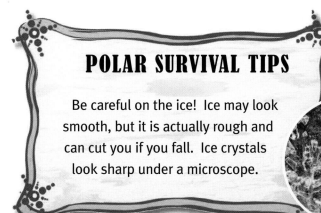

The Wildest Winds

Hurricane-force winds at the poles make life almost unbearable. Winds start and stop suddenly, too. One minute, you are leaning into the wind as you push forward through it. The next minute, the wind stops, and you fall flat on your face

Emperor penguin chicks huddle together in big groups to survive howling gales and temperatures of −76 °F (−60 °C).

The wind drives snow into every crack of your clothing. It even blows snow into your watch! The blowing snow causes **whiteouts**, which prevent you from seeing anything other than snow. Some explorers say a whiteout is like being inside a Ping-Pong ball!

Arctic explorers shelter in tents. During this storm, the winds reached 68 miles (110 km) per hour.

Arctic weather stations record temperature and wind speed.

Equipment can be hard to find in the snow. Here, flags mark their location.

Antarctica has the strongest winds in the world. In hilly areas, **katabatic** winds can blow at speeds up to 200 miles (320 km) per hour. They come in sudden blasts that can rip apart a tent.

In strong winds, your body loses heat quickly. For every extra 1.25 mile (2 km) per hour in wind speed, your body drops 1.8 °F (1 °C) in temperature. The drop in temperature due to wind is known as the **windchill factor**.

Polar Notebook

- Some polar explorers use **huskies** to pull their sleds.

- During a storm, a husky protects itself by curling into a tight ball with its back to the wind.

A husky's thick fur protects it during a blizzard.

- Huskies are stubborn and strong-willed. They have the determination to race and pull sleds long distances for hours.

POLAR SURVIVAL TIPS

If you want to get around the polar regions, huskies are the way to go! Many people feel safer riding dogsleds than driving snowmobiles because dogs do not break down in cold weather like machines do.

Deadly Seas

If you are sailing in polar waters, keep an eye out for danger. Storms can appear in an instant. Towering waves can toss a ship from side to side. You will also need to look out for icebergs.

All icebergs are dangerous to ships. They can be hard to see, especially in foggy conditions. An agency known as the International Ice Patrol protects ships in the Arctic. The agency tracks dangerous icebergs and warns ships of their position.

Only a small part of an iceberg rises above water.

A beluga whale's white color camouflages it among the icebergs of the Arctic Ocean.

In summer, the air above the Arctic Ocean is amazingly **humid**. It can feel wetter than a rain forest's air. Dense fog rises from the sea and wraps the ice in a thick, white blanket.

Ships in the Antarctic face foggy conditions.

Early Arctic Ocean explorers only had small boats, which put them at risk for whale attacks. Today, the opposite is true. Up to one-third of dead whales show signs of having been struck by ships.

Polar Notebook

- Icebergs drift at a speed of about 1,640 feet (500 m) per hour.

- Most icebergs melt fairly quickly. In 1926, however, one Arctic iceberg got within 155 miles (250 km) of the tropical island of Bermuda.

Bermuda is more than 2,490 miles (4,000 km) away from the Arctic.

- Ice can be noisy! In spring, the Arctic ice sounds like a construction site. The ice creaks and cracks as it shifts around.

POLAR SURVIVAL TIPS

Keep away from the edge of an **ice shelf**. These huge white cliffs can be dangerous. Giant chunks of ice can suddenly break off and fall onto your boat.

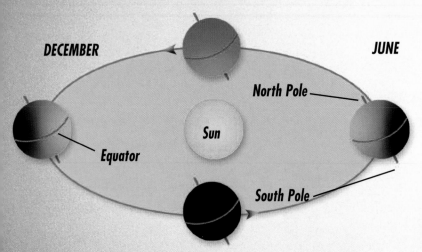

DECEMBER

JUNE

North Pole

Sun

Equator

South Pole

This diagram shows the way Earth's tilt affects light at the poles. In June, the North Pole tilts toward the Sun, so light falls on the Arctic for twenty-four hours each day. During that time, the South Pole tilts away from the Sun and remains in darkness. In December, the poles tilt in the opposite direction from the Sun.

The Longest Day

Can you imagine living in daylight for six months in a row? At the North and South poles, there is only one day and one night each year. Each day and each night lasts six months.

During the polar summer, the Sun comes close to the horizon, but it never actually sets. This ongoing sunlight is known as the midnight Sun. During winter, the Sun never rises. This ongoing darkness is known as the polar night.

If you lived in constant daylight or darkness, how would you divide the days? The reindeer that live in the Arctic do not have daily routines. They take naps whenever they feel tired.

During summer, the Sun is close to the horizon, but it will not set until winter.

During winter, **aurora** light fills the polar skies. These lights stretch hundreds of miles (kilometers) across the sky in a shimmering display of colors. In the north, the light is known as aurora borealis. In the south, it is known as aurora australis.

The aurora borealis is also known as the Northern Lights.

POLAR SURVIVAL TIPS

Fire is an important source of warmth and light in polar regions. Watch out, though! Fires burn fiercely in the dry polar air.

The Loneliest Place in the World

The polar landscape can be beautiful, peaceful, wild, and terrifying. It can also be very, very boring. Imagine being cooped up in a few small buildings for months on end with nowhere to go!

There are many **research stations** in the Antarctic. They have living, sleeping, and eating quarters as well as science laboratories and libraries. Some stations are built underground. They risk getting crushed by the weight of moving ice.

Scientists enter the Amundsen-Scott research station at the South Pole.

More researchers live in the Antarctic during summer than winter. Nearly two hundred people stay at the Amundsen-Scott station during summer, for example, but most leave in winter before the weather makes travel impossible.

POLAR SURVIVAL TIPS

Going for a walk? Make sure a survival rope is linked to the station and hang on to it. Without the rope, you can easily get lost.

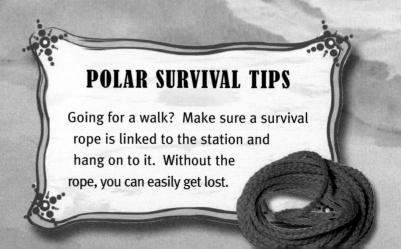

In 1911, Roald Amundsen (right) and Robert Falcon Scott raced each other to become the first explorers to reach the South Pole. The Amundsen-Scott research station is named in honor of both men.

Some Antarctic scientists study the ice or the plants in the region. Others look at weather conditions and pollution. The information they gather helps scientists around the world understand how the planet is changing as a result of **global warming**.

Polar Notebook

- Antarctica is far from other continents. The nearest large landmass is the southern tip of South America, which is more than 600 miles (960 km) away.

- The first Antarctic explorers arrived about two hundred years ago.

NASA astronaut

- Some NASA astronauts conduct part of their training in Antarctica. The long winters prepare them for dark, lonely journeys in space.

This plane is equipped with skis to land on the icy ground of the South Pole. It regularly brings supplies to scientists during the summer season.

FACT FILE:

Plant Survivors

Only the world's toughest plants can survive the fierce winds, freezing cold, and dark winter months of polar lands.

- During winter, both the Arctic and the Antarctic are barren, with almost no life.

- Moss, grass, **pearlwort, algae**, and **lichen** are the only plants that grow in the Antarctic.

Plants with berries, such as bearberries, are an important source of food for many Arctic animals.

- The Antarctic is so cold that plants grow very slowly. Moss grows as much in one year as your fingernails do in one week!

- The **tundra**, which is the land nearest the Arctic, bursts into life during the short summer.

Lichen grows on rocks.

- Arctic flowers grow quickly. They must bloom and produce seeds before the winter returns.

- Arctic plants are small and short and grow close together. The way they grow protects them from strong winds and extreme cold.

Dark leaves absorb sunlight better than pale leaves.

Arctic Plants

- **Arctic willows**
  - Arctic willows grow along the ground to avoid the wind.
  - They can grow more than 16 feet (5 m) long.
  - An arctic willow has branches that are never more than 4 inches (10 centimeters) above ground.

- **Arctic poppies**
  - A cup-shaped flower directs the Sun's rays toward the center of the arctic poppy's flower.
  - Due to their shape, these plants can stay warmer than the air around them.

- **Cotton grass**
  - Arctic winds blow cotton grass seeds far and wide.
  - In the Arctic, the Inuits use the silky "cotton" at the top of the plant to stuff pillows and mattresses.

Arctic willow

Arctic poppies

Cotton grass

- Some Arctic plants, such as the dwarf willow, are covered in tiny hairs that keep them warm.

- Some plants have dark flowers or leaves that absorb the Sun's heat.

The Arctic tundra blooms in summer.

This chart highlights the summer months in the Arctic and Antarctic.

ARCTIC	ANTARCTIC
JANUARY	JANUARY
FEBRUARY	FEBRUARY
MARCH	MARCH
APRIL	APRIL
MAY	MAY
JUNE	JUNE
JULY	JULY
AUGUST	AUGUST
SEPTEMBER	SEPTEMBER
OCTOBER	OCTOBER
NOVEMBER	NOVEMBER
DECEMBER	DECEMBER

Key: Winter =   Summer =

FACT FILE:

Arctic Animal Survivors

Animals do not live in the farthest northern region of the Arctic. The land and sea within the Arctic Circle are full of life, however. You can find reindeer, foxes, and lemmings on land and fish, seals, and whales in the sea.

An Arctic fox is white in winter.

- Large bodies hold in heat better than small ones. To stay warm, many polar animals are big, such as musk oxen and reindeer.

- Some Arctic animals have a thick layer of fat under their skin to keep them warm. This layer of fat is called blubber.

POLAR BEAR ADAPTATIONS TO THE ARCTIC

Hair sticks together when wet, making the coat waterproof

Powerful muscles for swimming long distances in search of seals to eat

Small ears so less skin is exposed to the cold

Thick blubber under the skin

Webbed feet for swimming

Arctic Survivors

- **Walrus**
  - This Arctic animal uses its long whiskers to feel for shellfish on the seabed.
  - Its tough head can knock a hole in ice that is up to 8 inches (20 cm) thick.

Walrus

- **Reindeer**
  - Both males and females have antlers. They use them to scrape snow away from the ground to find food.
  - Broad feet stop reindeer from sinking into the snow.

Reindeer

- **Arctic foxes**
  - Their thick, hairy foot pads grip the ice.
  - During autumn, their coat turns from brown to white so they can hide in the snow.

- **Lemmings**
  - These rodents dig a network of tunnels in the snow.
  - They live on plants they find beneath the snow.

Lemming

- During the winter months when it is hard to find food, animals can live off the blubber they have stored.

- Arctic animals, such as polar bears and foxes, have thick fur coats.

- Birds, such as snow geese, visit the Arctic tundra during summer to feed on the insects that breed there.

- Every summer, more than one million reindeer move north to the Arctic circle. There, they can feed day and night, thanks to the twenty-four hours of midnight Sun.

Walruses have so much blubber that they get too hot when they come on land!

FACT FILE:

Below the Antarctic Ice

Most of Antarctica is covered with ice. It is just too cold and dry for most animals to live here, but many creatures live in the ocean and on the ice close to the sea.

Krill grow up to 2 inches (6 cm) long. They feed on algae.

- Several species of birds have adapted to live in Antarctica. Colonies of penguins live along the rocky coastlines. Seabirds, such as petrels and skuas, hunt for fish here.

- Under the ice, the water is full of life. Fish, whales, crabs, and other creatures swim in the dark, cold depths.

- Cold water can hold more oxygen than warm water. Polar seas, therefore, have more oxygen than other ocean areas. All animals need oxygen, and the more oxygen an animal gets, the bigger it can grow. Some polar sea animals develop to giant sizes!

- Orcas are the largest predators in Antarctic waters. They are clever hunters, too. An orca will tip up small icebergs to knock resting seals into the water. Then it will snap them up.

Orcas prefer cooler waters. They live in both the Arctic and Antarctic.

Monsters of the Deep

- **Giant woodlice**
  - These creatures grow up to 8 inches (20 cm) long.
  - They are scavengers and eat the remains of any dead animal they come across.

Giant woodlouse

- **Sea spiders**
  - Giant sea spiders live in deep Antarctic waters and feed on sea anemones.
  - Bright orange in color, they have ten to twelve legs.
  - Antarctic sea spiders weigh up to one thousand times as much as sea spiders in warmer waters, and they can grow to the size of a dinner plate.

Sea spider

- **Ice fish**
  - These fish make their own **antifreeze** that allows their blood to stay liquid when most other animal bodies would freeze solid.
  - They have large eyes that help them hunt in the dark.

Ice fish

- **Weddell seals**
  - Weddell seals spend long periods of time under the ice.
  - To keep air holes open for breathing, they gnaw the ice with their teeth.
  - They can stay under water for up to seventy minutes and can dive to depths of 1,903 feet (580 m).

Weddell seal

- During summer, Antarctic seas are filled with shrimplike creatures called krill.

- Lake Vostok lies in the heart of the Antarctic, buried under 2 miles (4 km) of ice. The water in the lake is cold and very dark.

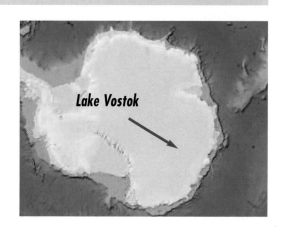
Lake Vostok

25

FACT FILE:

Arctic People

Even today, nobody lives in the Antarctic for more than a few years at a time. People have made their homes in the Arctic, however, for about fifteen thousand years.

WHERE ARCTIC PEOPLE LIVE

PEOPLE	COUNTRY
EVENKS	RUSSIA
INUITS	GREENLAND, CANADA, ALASKA, AND RUSSIA
NENETS	RUSSIA
SAMI	NORWAY, SWEDEN, FINLAND, AND RUSSIA

ARCTIC CIRCLE

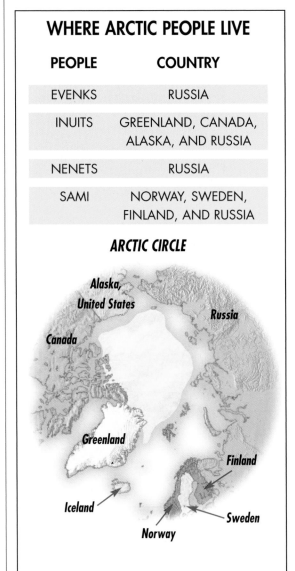

A Sami woman walks among a herd of reindeer.

- Many groups of peoples live in the Arctic, including the Inuits and Nenets. Each group has its own language and customs.

- The Inuits hunt many animals, including walruses, polar bears, reindeer, seals, and geese. The people use these animals for food, shelter, clothing, and weapons.

- Long ago, the Inuits made seal skin boots and lined them with moss and dry grass for extra **insulation**.

Survival Techniques

- **Igloos**
    - Igloos are temporary shelters that can be quickly built from ice.
    - They are surprisingly warm inside.
    - Their inner walls are covered in snow, which melts and then freezes into a smooth layer of ice.

- **Snow glare**
    - Goggles protect your eyes from the glare of snow.
    - In the past, Inuits made goggles from reindeer skin.

- **Balanced diet**
    - Early Arctic explorers often suffered from scurvy, which is an illness that comes from not getting enough vitamin C.
    - In the past, Inuits ate raw meat, which contains vitamin C.

Igloo

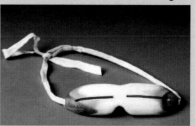

Reindeer-skin goggles

Raw seal meat contains Vitamin C.

- The Nenets and Sami people traditionally followed giant herds of reindeer across the Arctic and used the animals for their meat and milk, which they made cheese from. They made warm clothes and other goods from the reindeer. Tents made from the skins were light and easy to carry.

- Today, most Arctic people use snowmobiles for transportation and live in modern houses with central heating.

Traditional Sami clothing is red and blue and decorated with yellow or white.

FACT FILE:

Poles in Danger

In the last few decades, the world has become warmer. Global warming is melting polar ice. The shrinking polar ice makes life difficult for polar animals, particularly those in the Arctic.

Without enough polar ice, reindeer cannot walk to their traditional feeding places in the Arctic.

- Although the poles are at the far ends of the world, people are having a big effect on them. Pollution is spreading to the polar regions and damaging polar ice.

- Sea ice is melting earlier in the year than usual. Without large sheets of ice to travel over, polar bears have a hard time reaching the seals, their main source of food.

- If the polar ice melted completely, the seas would rise by 164 feet (50 m). They would flood the coasts. Many large cities would be affected, including London, New York, Mumbai in India, and Tokyo, Japan.

- The poles are a good place to study our planet because they are so clean. Any pollution can be measured easily.

Arctic summer in 1979

Arctic summer in 2005

These pictures show the Arctic ice cover in 1979 and 2005. They show how much ice has melted during that time.

Polar Problems

- ## Changing the environment

  - Drilling for oil brings roads, houses, and pipelines into the Arctic.

  - These structures can block the traditional routes that reindeer use for moving across the Arctic.

  - The change in reindeer behavior affects the animals that hunt them, such as wolves.

  - A damaged oil pipe can spill millions of gallons (liters) of oil, killing hundreds of birds, fish, and mammals.

- ## Overfishing

  - People and companies take large numbers of fish and squid from the polar seas.

  - Overfishing reduces the food source for animals, such as dolphins, seals, and penguins.

Oil pipes in Alaska

Oil spills kill wildlife

Overfishing

- No one owns Antarctica, but forty countries around the world have agreed to protect the continent.

- The 1961 Antarctic Treaty allows all scientists to work in Antarctica, but only if they do not conduct tests that would harm the environment.

- Strict laws for scientists and tourists in polar areas help to protect the **unique** habitat.

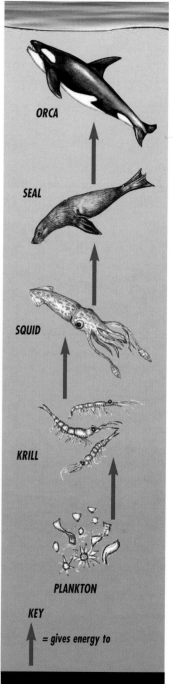

ORCA

SEAL

SQUID

KRILL

PLANKTON

KEY

↑ = gives energy to

This simple food chain shows how larger creatures depend on smaller creatures for food. If pollution affects one link in the chain, it can harm many other animals.

Glossary

algae — tiny, simple plants that live in water

Antarctic — the area surrounding the South Pole. Antarctica is a continent.

antifreeze — something that stops a liquid, such as blood, from freezing

Arctic — the area within the Arctic Circle. Most of the Arctic is sea and ice, but there is some land, including parts of Russia, Canada, Greenland, and Alaska.

Arctic Ocean — the ocean around the Arctic. Much of the sea is covered by ice.

astronomers — people who study outer space

aurora — a glow in the sky caused by particles from the Sun reacting to Earth's atmosphere

dehydration — a condition caused by not having enough water

elevation — the height above sea level at which a land formation, such as a mountain, is measured

equator — an imaginary line around Earth, dividing the world into a northern half and southern half

global warming — the increase in Earth's temperature caused by pollution in the atmosphere

humid — containing a large amount of water vapor in the air

huskies — dogs that belong to a breed that is adapted to survive in polar conditions

icebergs — large masses of ice floating in the water

ice shelf — a sheet of ice that forms over water and is attached to land

insulation — a material that is used to protect something from the cold

katabatic — strong winds that blow down a mountain

lichen — a simple plant that grows on rocks and takes its nutrients from the air

magnetic North Pole — the place where compass needles point. It is caused by the shape of Earth's magnetic fields. The magnetic North Pole is not in the same place as the true North Pole.

mirages — tricks of the light that cause you to see things that are not there

North Pole — the point on Earth that is farthest north

pearlwort — a plant that looks like moss

plankton — plants and animals that are so small that each one can only be seen with a microscope

research stations — buildings where scientists live and work

sea level — the height of the sea's surface when it is midway between high and low tide. It is used as a starting point for measuring the height of mountains or other landforms.

snowblindness — damage to the eyes caused by the glare of the Sun on bright white snow

South Pole — the point on Earth that is farthest south

stilts — long, strong poles that support something above the ground

tundra — the vast, flat land in the Arctic, where it is too cold for any trees to grow

unique — different from most other things

whiteouts — weather conditions, such as a heavy snow blizzard, that allow you to only see white

windchill factor — the temperature that you feel, which is a result of the combination of air temperature and wind speed

For Further Information

Books

The Arctic. Our Wild World Ecosystems (series). Wayne Lynch (Northword Press)

Polar Habitats. Exploring Habitats (series). Barbara Taylor (Gareth Stevens Publishing)

Polar Regions. Caring for the Planet (series). Neil Champion (Smart Apple Media)

Web Sites

Enchanted Learning: Arctic Animals.
www.enchantedlearning.com/coloring/arcticanimals.shtml
Click on the links to find out more about Arctic animals.

Inuit Life in Nunavik.
kativik.net/ulluriaq/Nunavik/inuitlife
Click on links to find out about a day in the life of an Inuit child and more.

Publisher's note to educators and parents: Our editors have carefully reviewed these Web sites to ensure that they are suitable for children. Many Web sites change frequently, however, and we cannot guarantee that a site's future contents will continue to meet our high standards of quality and educational value. Be advised that children should be closely supervised whenever they access the Internet.

Index